———— Fold in the reverse direction of the dotted line. This is known as the 'mountain' fold.

———— Fold along the dotted line in the direction of the arrow. This is called the 'valley' fold.

—— Cut

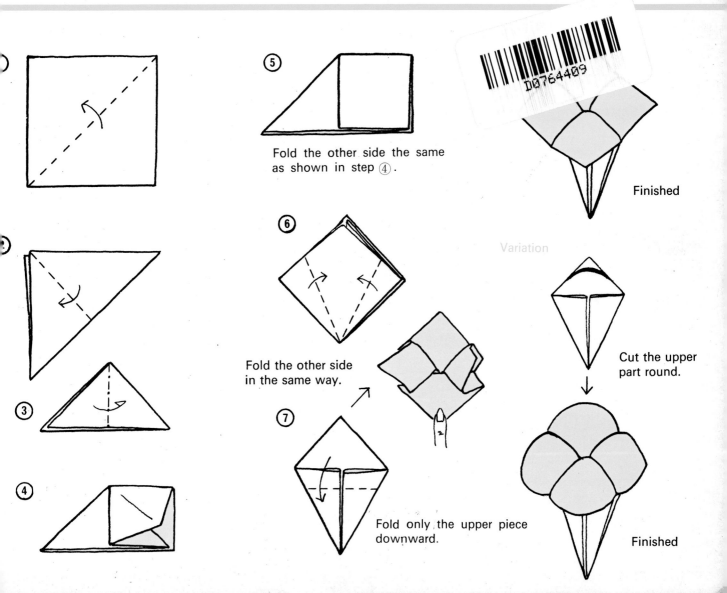

⑤ Fold the other side the same as shown in step ④.

⑥ Fold the other side in the same way.

⑦ Fold only the upper piece downward.

Finished

Variation

Cut the upper part round.

Finished

BALLOON

①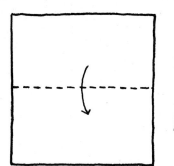

②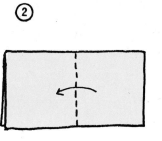

③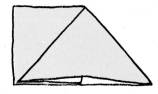

④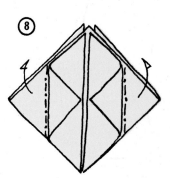

⑤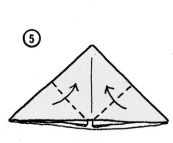

⑥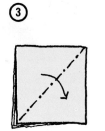

⑦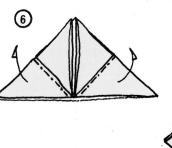

⑧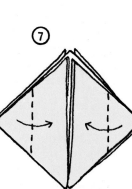

⑨

⑩

Slide each head into pockets and blow up the folded balloon through a hole.

Have a fun with the balloon by folding it with newspapers or large wrapping paper.

Fold the other side in the same way.

Finished

AIRPLANE

Use a paper cut in three-fourths.

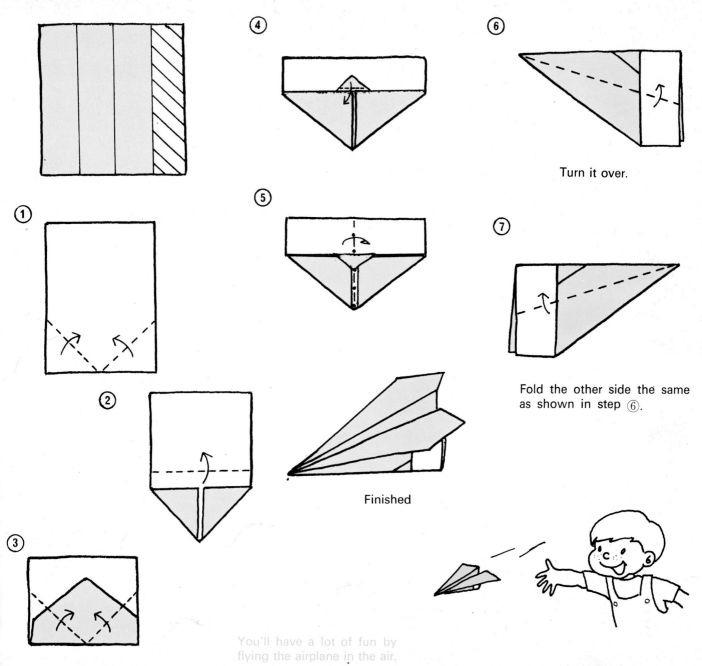

④

⑥

Turn it over.

①

⑤

⑦

②

Finished

Fold the other side the same
as shown in step ⑥.

③

You'll have a lot of fun by
flying the airplane in the air.

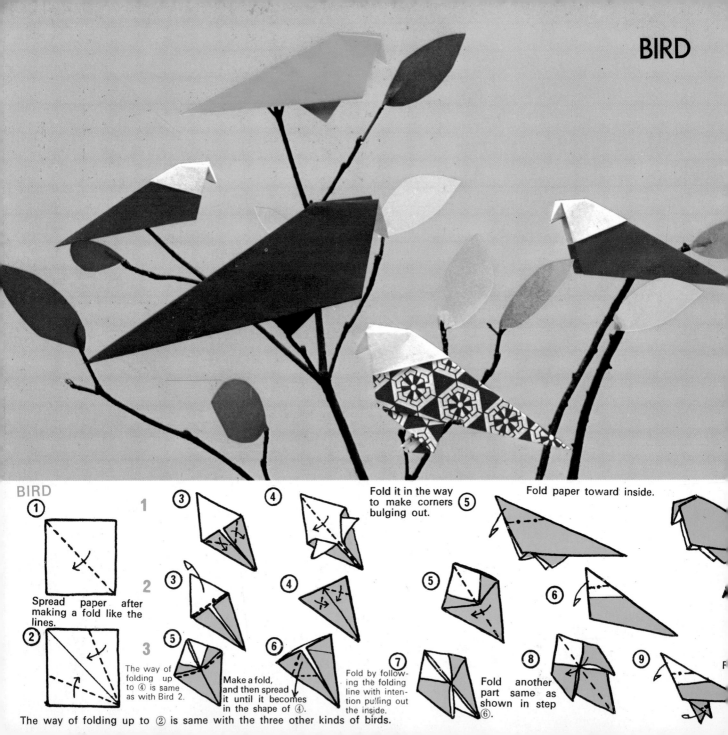

BIRD

BIRD

① Spread paper after making a fold like the lines.

② The way of folding up to ② is same with the three other kinds of birds.

③ ④

⑤ The way of folding up to ④ is same as with Bird 2.

⑥ Make a fold, and then spread it until it becomes in the shape of ④.

1

2

3 ③ ④

⑦ Fold by following the folding line with intention pulling out the inside.

⑧ Fold another part same as shown in step ⑥.

⑨

Fold it in the way to make corners bulging out. ⑤

Fold paper toward inside.

⑤ ⑥

AQUATIC BIRD

JATIC BIRD The way of folding up to ② is same with the three other kinds of birds.

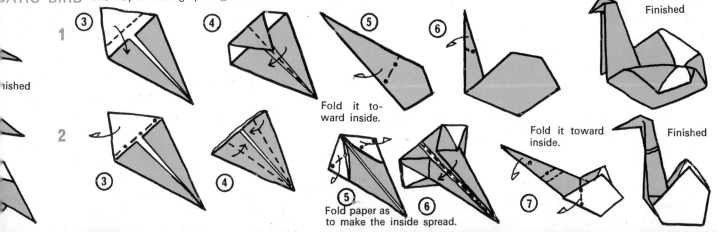

1 ③ ④ ⑤ Fold it toward inside. ⑥ Finished

nished

2 ③ ④ ⑤ Fold paper as to make the inside spread. ⑥ Fold it toward inside. ⑦ Finished

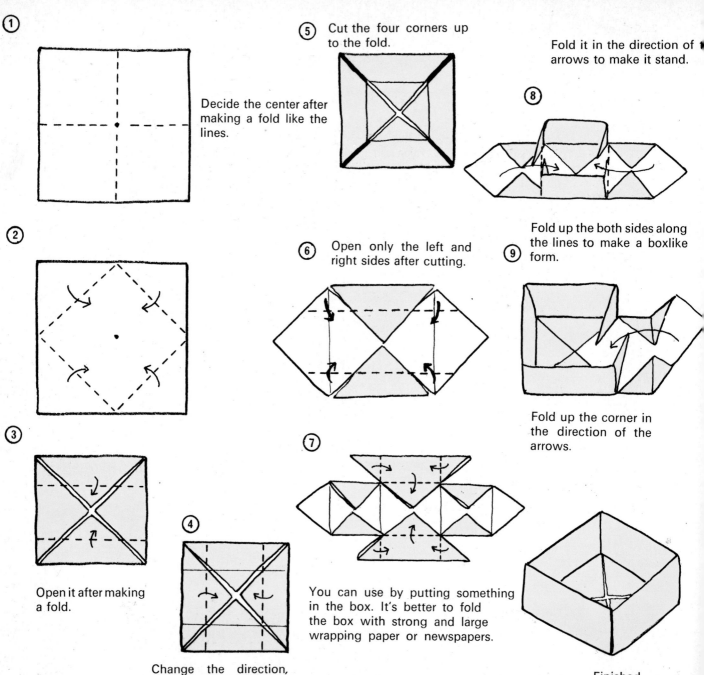

① Decide the center after making a fold like the lines.

②

③ Open it after making a fold.

④ Change the direction, and make a fold same as shown in step ③.

⑤ Cut the four corners up to the fold.

⑥ Open only the left and right sides after cutting.

⑦ You can use by putting something in the box. It's better to fold the box with strong and large wrapping paper or newspapers.

Fold it in the direction of arrows to make it stand.

⑧

Fold up the both sides along the lines to make a boxlike form.

⑨

Fold up the corner in the direction of the arrows.

Finished

BOX

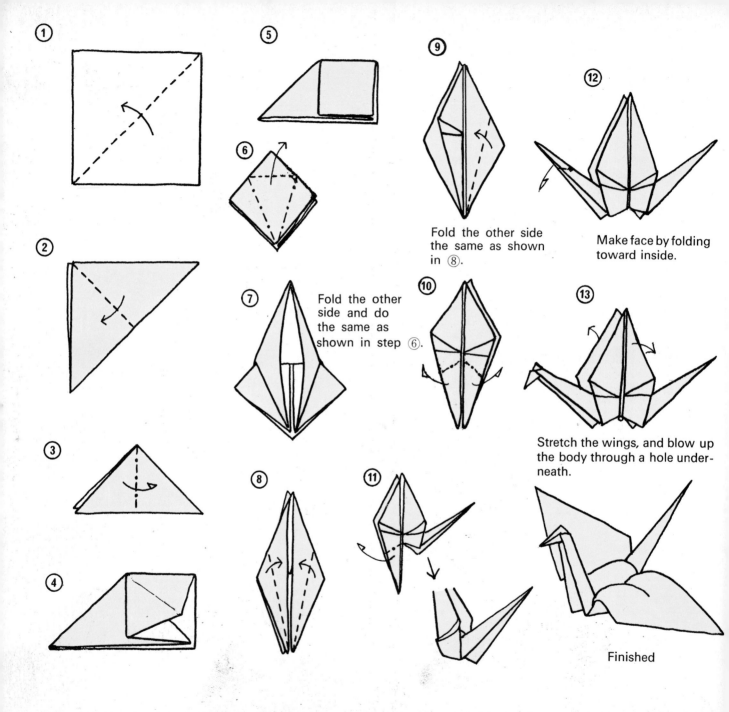

①

⑤

⑨
Fold the other side
the same as shown
in ⑧.

⑫
Make face by folding
toward inside.

②

⑥

⑦
Fold the other
side and do
the same as
shown in step ⑥.

⑩

⑬
Stretch the wings, and blow up
the body through a hole under-
neath.

③

④

⑧

⑪

Finished

STORK

TORTOISE and JUMPING-FROG

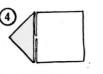

Use a slender paper cut in half.

①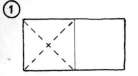

Spread it after making a fold like the lines.

②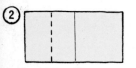

Turn over the paper and make a fold like the line.

③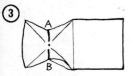

Turn it over again.

Put A and B lines together for folding.

④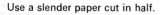

The right side must be folded in a triangle the same as the left side.

⑤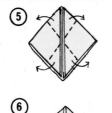

⑥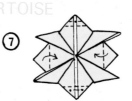

The way of folding "Tortoise" and "Jumping-frog" is the same up to step ⑥.

TORTOISE

⑦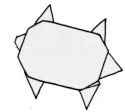

Finished

JUMPING-FROG

Change the direction of step ⑥.

⑦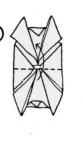

⑧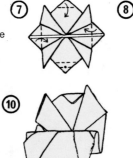

⑨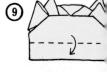

⑩

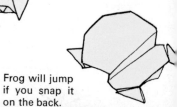

Frog will jump if you snap it on the back.

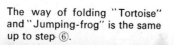